Dear Parent:
Your child's love of reading starts here!

Every child learns to read in a different way and at his or her own speed. Some go back and forth between reading levels and read favorite books again and again. Others read through each level in order. You can help your young reader improve and become more confident by encouraging his or her own interests and abilities. From books your child reads with you to the first books he or she reads alone, there are I Can Read Books for every stage of reading:

SHARED READING
Basic language, word repetition, and whimsical illustrations, ideal for sharing with your emergent reader

BEGINNING READING
Short sentences, familiar words, and simple concepts for children eager to read on their own

READING WITH HELP
Engaging stories, longer sentences, and language play for developing readers

READING ALONE
Complex plots, challenging vocabulary, and high-interest topics for the independent reader

ADVANCED READING
Short paragraphs, chapters, and exciting themes for the perfect bridge to chapter books

I Can Read Books have introduced children to the joy of reading since 1957. Featuring award-winning authors and illustrators and a fabulous cast of beloved characters, I Can Read Books set the standard for beginning readers.

A lifetime of discovery begins with the magical words "I Can Read!"

Visit www.icanread.com for information
on enriching your child's reading experience.

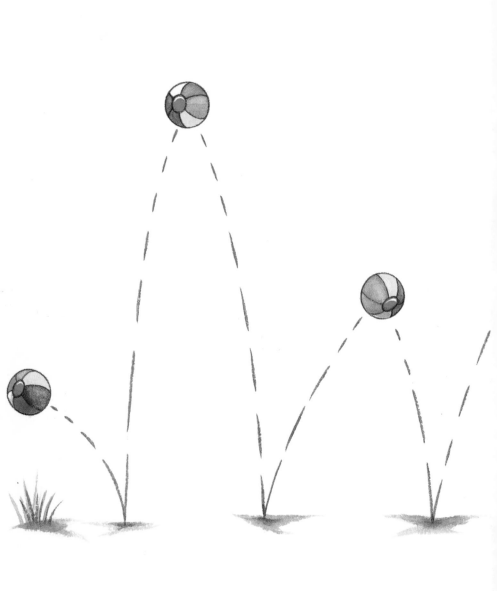

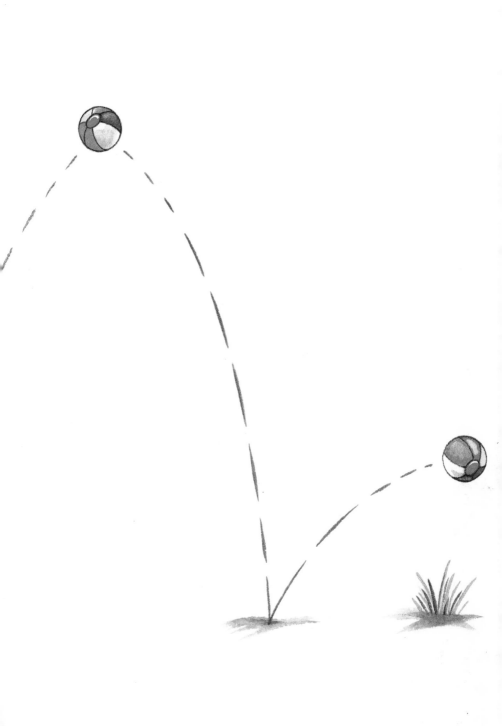

I Can Read!™

SHARED
My
First
READING

Biscuit's New Trick

story by ALYSSA SATIN CAPUCILLI
pictures by PAT SCHORIES

HarperCollins®, ♣®, and I Can Read Book® are trademarks of HarperCollins Publishers Inc.

Library of Congress Cataloging-in-Publication Data
Capucilli, Alyssa.
  Biscuit's new trick / story by Alyssa Satin Capucilli ; pictures by Pat Schories.
    p.   cm.—(A my first I can read book)
  Summary: A puppy does all sorts of tricks in the process of learning the one his master is trying to teach him.
  ISBN-10: 0-06-028067-0 (trade bdg.) — ISBN-13: 978-0-06-028067-3 (trade bdg.)
  ISBN-10: 0-06-028068-9 (lib. bdg.) — ISBN-13: 978-0-06-028068-0 (lib. bdg.)
  ISBN-10: 0-06-444308-6 (pbk.) — ISBN-13: 978-0-06-444308-1 (pbk.)
  [1. Dogs—Training—Fiction.] I. Schories, Pat, ill. II. Title. III. Series.
Pz7.C179Biu 2000   99-23004
[E]—dc21   CIP
                                                                                                                    AC

❖
09 10 11 12 13 SCP 30 29 28 27 26

For Anthony and Ruby, the newest
—A.S.C.

To Laura
—P.S.

Here, Biscuit!

Look what I have.

Woof, woof!

It's time to learn
a new trick, Biscuit.
Woof, woof!

It's time to learn
to fetch the ball.
Ready?

Fetch the ball, Biscuit.

Woof, woof!

Silly puppy!

Don't roll over now.

Get the ball, Biscuit.

Fetch the ball, Biscuit.

Woof, woof!

Where are you going,

Biscuit?

Woof!

Funny puppy!
Fetch the ball,
not your bone.

Let's try again.

Fetch the ball, Biscuit!

Woof, woof!

Good puppy!
You got the ball.
Woof!

Wait, Biscuit.

16

Bring the ball back!

Woof, woof!

Let's try one more time.

Fetch the ball, Biscuit!

Woof, woof!

Oh no!
Not in the mud!

Stop, Biscuit!

Don't fetch it now!

Woof!

Oh, Biscuit!

23

You did it!

You learned a new trick!

Woof, woof!

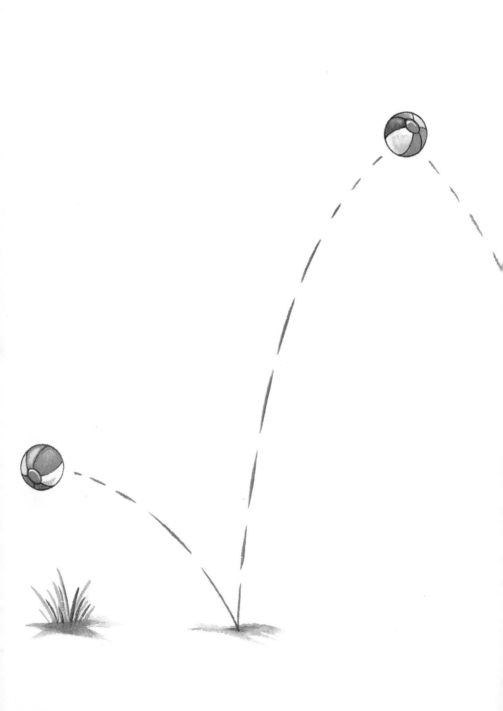

THE BOY FRIEND

SANDY WILSON

THE BOY FRIEND

A Play in Three Acts

★

With a Preface by Vida Hope

and

Illustrations by the Author

E. P. DUTTON & COMPANY, INC.

NEW YORK, 1955

INDIVIDUAL COPYRIGHTS

TO
"THE BOY FRIEND" COMPANY
IN
LONDON and NEW YORK
WITH
LOVE and GRATITUDE

ACT I

The Drawing Room of the Villa Caprice, Madame Dubonnet's
Finishing School, near Nice — Morning

Page 25

ACT II

The Plage — That Afternoon

Page 57

ACT III

The Terrasse of the Café Pataplon — The same night

Page 95

TIME: 1926

"The Boy Friend" was presented in New York City at the Royale Theatre on September 30, 1954, when the cast was as follows:

HORTENSE	*Paulette Girard*
NANCY	*Millicent Martin*
MAISIE	*Ann Wakefield*
FAY	*Stella Claire*
DULCIE	*Dilys Lay*
POLLY	*Julie Andrews*
MARCEL	*Joe Milan*
ALPHONSE	*Buddy Schwab*
PIERRE	*Jerry Newby*
MADAME DUBONNET	*Ruth Altman*
BOBBY VAN HUSEN	*Bob Scheerer*
PERCIVAL BROWNE	*Eric Berry*
TONY	*John Hewer*
PHILLIPE	*Jimmy Alex*
MONICA	*Berkley Marsh*
LORD BROCKHURST	*Geoffrey Hibbert*
LADY BROCKHURST	*Moyna MacGill*
SUSANNE	*Lyn Connorty*
GUESTS	*Phoebe MacKay* *Marge Ellis* *Mickey Calin*
GENDARME	*Douglas Deane*
WAITER	*Lyn Robert*
PEPE	*Joe Milan*
LOLITA	*Stella Claire*

PRODUCED BY FEUER AND MARTIN
Production by VIDA HOPE
Dances arranged by JOHN HEAWOOD
Settings and Costumes by REGINALD WOOLLEY
New York Production Supervising Designers:
Scenery and Lighting by FEDER
Costumes by ROBERT MACKINTOSH

PREFACE

WHEN a 'miracle' show occurs, usually not more than once in a decade or even longer, people are inclined to have lengthy post mortems and ask why? Why is it such a success? The only other 'miracle' shows I remember are *Journey's End* — a small play with unknown actors that suddenly seized London by the throat and then went on to grip the entire world, and *Oklahoma!* — the American musical which began life in a Boston theatre as an 'intimate' show (forecast by the press there as a failure) and then proceeded to rocket round the universe and change the entire shape and form of light musical entertainment. Now has come *The Boy Friend,* gaily playing to capacity in London and New York as I write these words, and due to open shortly in most of the major cities in other continents as well. Why? What makes it so successful? As the person most closely associated with it apart from the author, I'm afraid the answer is I just don't know. I have theories of course, but frankly I am not at all sure that they are right. Like the audiences in the theatre I just fell in love with it and remained in love.

When Sandy asked me to write this preface for him, I asked him what sort of thing I should write, and he said in his shy way 'I think people would like to know how we did it.' So here, then, is the answer to his request.

Early in 1953 my very good friends the Players Theatre asked me if I would produce a new small musical by Sandy Wilson, and having accepted I went round to Sandy's flat one bleak February morning to look at the book and hear the music. He was no stranger to me as I had already produced a late-night revue that he had written previously, and we had found we got on well together. He looked pale, seemed over-anxious that I should like it, and, as always when he is nervous, played his own composition shockingly. But never mind; I saw, I heard, and I was conquered. Over coffee I declared my love for *The Boy Friend*, told Sandy I wanted to do it as a serious reproduction of a period and not a burlesque, and from that moment on his whole demeanour brightened and a friendship was forged that has withstood all the vicissitudes of the various productions of the show.

We started rehearsing in March, and I well remember haranguing a rather young company that we were to present a show that would be witty, elegant, charming and tender, and that in no circumstances would I tolerate any attitude of laughing at the Twenties. They listened politely then went away and had their lunch, when no doubt they expounded on the lunacy of their producer and their crack-brained author. But it worked, and within less than a week the cast were even more in love with the show than we were, and were telling each other off for any hint of over-playing or burlesque business.

We all did a tremendous amount of research. My mother, who was an actress, gave me the exact formula for make-up in that era; the cast found old books of photographs and fashion drawings; and the Players Theatre management, charming and considerate as always, produced for me some copies of *Play Pictorial*—a monthly magazine of the Twenties which gave a complete pictorial record of the successes of that time such as *No! No! Nanette!* and *Mercenary Mary*. From these invaluable photographs I took my groupings for the ensemble work, and the girls in the show were taught stance, posture, gesture and so on. Reggie Woolley designed the most entrancing sets and costumes, all of which helped us really to 'live' the period again. I asked for John Heawood to do my choreography. He was not then known as a dance director, but I knew him as an old friend and fabulous dancer himself with a sense of style in hitting a step of the period that is almost matchless. So imbued with our show were we, that inspiration started coming, it seemed as if by magic. For instance when the hero and heroine sing 'A Room in Bloomsbury' in Act 2, I suddenly took it into my head that they should do a repeat chorus without singing the words, but in mime. This is always one of the hits of the evening, and stars like the delectable and witty Binnie Hale have asked me how I *knew*—that was what they *always* did in such a number. Well, how *did* I know? I cannot claim any credit for it — it just happened.

There were two things I was very grateful for. One was the unfailing help and complete and utter freedom the Players management gave me. And the other was Sandy himself. He very rarely came to rehearsals, unless I particularly asked for him. His implicit trust and faith in me to carry out his intentions in a proper manner was something I shall always treasure. We seemed to have a most extraordinary *rapport* over *The Boy Friend*, which remains to this day. It is not unusual in the theatre for author and producer to be justifiably suspicious of each other and have their little quarrels over interpretation or presentation, but over *The Boy Friend*—never. We both knew what we were aiming at and we have watched over the child from birth, Sandy as father and mother, and myself as some old auntie who gets the child ready for the party.

When the final dress rehearsal arrived, we were in more of a flutter than is customary. Not only was there the usual flurry, with nerves and disturbances (we had an undue amount of illness during rehearsals—at one period the entire cast had German measles but manfully worked on—as we *all* had it there was no question of infecting others!), but we were all so dizzy with love for our show that we couldn't bear the possibility of anyone not liking it. But all was well—they *did* like it, and the rest is theatrical history that needs no further explanation.

So that is the story of how we did it. And here for you to read is the very play I saw that February morning. I wonder will your reaction be the same as mine? I think it will, for here in Sandy's writing is a tenderness that catches the heart as well as the period dialogue that seems so funny and fatuous to present-day audiences. And added to that are his delightful sketches to embellish it.

I am delighted that Sandy asked me to write the preface to his book; partly because we have been so closely associated over this show, and partly because I can now record in black and white my gratitude to every single person connected with the original production, all of whom gave much more than was asked or necessary to their individual jobs or performances.

But perhaps the chief reason for my pleasure is that the creation of *The Boy Friend* in the theatre gave me some of the greatest thrills and fun in my life.

Thank you, Sandy.

VIDA HOPE

AUTHOR'S NOTE

As I look through this published version of *The Boy Friend*, I am reminded of an observation made by Noel Coward in the preface to his Collected *Sketches and Lyrics*. He said that, while the sketches made reasonably good reading, some of the lyrics might appear rather baffling, divorced from their tunes, but he assured his readers that 'Although they may not appear to scan on paper, they scan all right when fitted to the music.' May I echo Mr. Coward with reference to the lyrics included in this book? To some of its readers I hope a few of the melodies may be familiar, but I would like to crave the indulgence of those who have not seen the show and suggest, as Mr. Coward did, that they make up their own tunes!

The question I am most frequently asked about *The Boy Friend* is: 'How did you know, at your age, what the shows of the nineteen-twenties were like?' In truth I believe that people who have not met me imagine I am three old men. The fact is that, though only an infant at the time, I was surrounded by elder sisters and their friends who were constantly learning the Charleston and playing 'Tea for Two' and 'Lady be Good' on an old cabinet gramophone. In fact I used to refuse to go to bed until one of my sisters had played me the record of a song entitled 'Do Shrimps Make Good Mothers?' As I grew older and the twenties gave way to the thirties, I still looked back on the period with great fondness and I can clearly recollect, while at my prep school, trying to remember how the tune of the Charleston went. Later on, at least five years before *The Boy Friend* was thought of, I would lose no opportunity of seeing touring revivals of nineteen-twenties musicals and buying sheet music of the period at second-hand music dealers. So by the time the Players' Theatre asked me to write the show, there was no need for research. I seemed to know all about it, and everything came tumbling out on paper as if it had been waiting to be written.

The fact that so many other people seem to look upon the period of *The Boy Friend* with the same fondness as myself, regardless of their age, has given me enormous pleasure. But I would like to make it clear, here and now, that this show was never intended as a 'reply to *Oklahoma!*' or indeed to any of the very successful and essentially modern American musicals. I feel that the English Theatre has very far to go before it can rival Broadway in this field. *The Boy Friend* is simply a loving salute to those far-off days of cloche hat and the short skirt, a valentine from one post-war period to another. To write it, to see it come to life, and to watch it achieve success was for me a wonderful and, I believe, unique experience.

Sandy Wilson

ACT ONE

ACT ONE

¶ *The Drawing Room of the Villa Caprice, Madame Dubonnet's Finishing School on the outskirts of Nice. At the back, French windows opening on to the garden, with a view of the sea beyond.*

As the curtain rises HORTENSE, *a chic French maid, is on the 'phone*

HORTENSE

'Allo, 'allo! Is that Monsieur Gaston, the costumier? 'Ere is Madame Dubonnet's maid. Dubonnet. D-U-B-O-N-N-E-T . . . Madame Dubonnet of the Villa Caprice, the school for young ladies . . . I wish to know if you 'ave ready the costume for Miss Polly Browne. Browne. B-R-O-W-N avec E . . . with an E . . . she wishes it for the carnival ball ce soir. . . .

The door L. flies open and in rush MAISIE, DULCIE, FAY *and* NANCY; *four extremely pretty girls in summer frocks and hats. They carry dress and hat boxes and are in a state of extreme animation.* HORTENSE *rings off.*

HORTENSE

Mam'selles! Mam'selles! Silence, s'il vous plait! 'Ave you forgotten who you are?

THE GIRLS

Forgotten who we are? Of course not!

We're perfect young ladies
Preparing to take
Our places among the noblesse.

We're perfect young ladies
Preparing to make
The most of the charms we possess.

We're being finished,
And our families' wealth
May be diminished,
But at least we all have perfect health.

And making the grade is
Our duty, you see,
For perfect young ladies are we.

*   *   *

We're perfect young ladies
Who hope to attract
A husband whose credit is good.

HORTENSE

You may be young ladies,
But why don't you act
The way that a young lady should?

I've often told you——

GIRLS

Please don't tell us again.

HORTENSE

I ought to scold you——

GIRLS

But you know it
Would be quite in vain.

For being our maid is
Your duty, you see . . .
For perfect young ladies are——

HORTENSE

Perfect young ladies. Hm!

GIRLS

Perfect young ladies are we.

In the course of the number HORTENSE *relieves them of their boxes and* EXITS. *The number ends and the girls giggle excitedly.*

DULCIE

Oh, I can't wait for this evening! My frock is a dream!

FAY

So is mine! And rather daring too! I'm sure Madame Dubonnet will be furious!

MAISIE

Not she! I bet you she'll turn up in something frightfully shocking! [*They all laugh*]

DULCIE

Do you think we shall be allowed out late?

MAISIE

Who cares? I intend to dance the whole night through!

FAY

Do you, Maisie? Who with?

MAISIE

Anyone who asks me!

DULCIE

Don't take any notice of her, girls. She'll dance all night with Bobby Van Husen, that terribly rich and good-looking American who's staying at the Negresco! [*Laughter*]

MAISIE

Oh, no, I shan't. He bores me! [*She goes to the windows*]

NANCY

Oh, isn't she the limit!

DULCIE

No wonder they call her Madcap Maisie!

MAISIE

Oh, look, here comes Polly Browne, across the tennis court.

FAY, DULCIE and NANCY

Polly Browne?

MAISIE

Yes. She's carrying a letter. [*She waves*] Hullo, Polly!

FAY, DULCIE and NANCY

[*Joining her*] Hullo, Polly!

POLLY ENTERS. *She is a sweet girl in a simple frock with no jewelry. She carries a letter.*

POLLY

Oh, hullo everyone! Where have you been?

MAISIE

We dashed into town to get our costumes for the Carnival Ball! We couldn't wait until Monsieur Gaston delivered them!

FAY

You must see mine, Polly! You'll adore it!

DULCIE

And mine! You'll be green with envy!

MAISIE

Oh, be quiet, chaps. You know we'll all be jealous of Polly when she gets hers. What are you going as, Polly?

POLLY

I'm going as Pierrette.

FAY, DULCIE, MAISIE and NANCY

Pierrette! How divine!

MAISIE

Now do tell us your secret, Polly.

POLLY

What secret?

MAISIE

Well, if you're going as Pierrette, who's going to be Pierrot?

POLLY

Oh—I still want it to be a secret.

THE GIRLS

Oh, Polly!

POLLY

But—I've had another letter. From Paris.

FAY

From Paris! How marvellous!

POLLY

[*Reading letter*] He says he's motoring down overnight; in fact he should be here any moment now.

DULCIE

Oh, how thrilling!

FAY

And how does he sign himself? Does he say 'Passionately yours'?

MAISIE

Or 'Yours adoringly'?

DULCIE

Or does he just say 'With all my love'?

THE GIRLS

Oh, do tell us about him, Polly!

POLLY

Well, there really isn't very much to tell. I expect you know how
I feel as well as I do . . .

> Any girl who's reached the age
> Of seventeen or thereabouts
> Has but one desire in view.
> She knows she has reached the stage
> Of needing one to care about;
> Nothing else will really do.

DULCIE

Childhood games are left behind,

FAY

And her heart takes wing,

MAISIE

Hoping that it soon will find

GIRLS

Just one thing.

POLLY

We've got to have
We plot to have

For it's so dreary not to have
That certain thing called the Boy Friend.

POLLY and GIRLS

We scheme about
And dream about
And we've been known to scream about
That certain thing called the Boy Friend.

POLLY

He is really a necessity
If you want to get on.
And we might as well confess it, he
Is our *sine qua non*.

POLLY and GIRLS

We sigh for him
And cry for him
And we would gladly die for him
That certain thing called the Boy Friend.

We plead to have
We need to have
In fact our poor hearts bleed to have
That certain thing called the Boy Friend.

We'd save for him
And slave for him
We'd even misbehave for him
That certain thing called the Boy Friend

BOYS

Life without us is quite impossible
And devoid of all charms.
No amount of idle gossip'll
Keep them out of our arms.

POLLY and GIRLS

We're blue without
Can't do without
Our dreams just won't come true without
That certain thing called the Boy Friend.

DULCIE

Boys, boys, you know you're not allowed on the premises! You must leave at once! [BOYS EXEUNT] But you still haven't told us much about him, Polly!

FAY

Not even his Christian name——

NANCY

What is it, Polly?

POLLY

Well, it's er—it's er——

MAISIE

Cave, girls, here's Madame Dubonnet.

ENTER MADAME DUBONNET R. *She is a striking-looking lady in her forties, severely but smartly dressed. She carries a bouquet and single rose.*

MME. DUBONNET

Tiens! Tiens! mes enfants! This is no way to behave. Away all of you to your classroom! Mademoiselle Alice is waiting to instruct you in petit point.

THE GIRLS

Oui, Madame Dubonnet. [*They curtsey and* EXEUNT, POLLY *going last*]

MME. DUBONNET

Mam'selle Browne!

POLLY

Yes, Madame Dubonnet?

MME. DUBONNET

I wish to have a little word with you, ma petite. Will you close the door?

POLLY

Yes, Madame. [*She does so*]

MME. DUBONNET

Do not be frightened, ma chère. You have done nothing wrong. I simply wish to ask you if you are coming to the Ball tonight?

POLLY

Oh! yes, of course. I've ordered my frock. I'm going as Pierrette.

MME. DUBONNET

So? You have a friend to take you, hein?

POLLY

Oh, yes. I had a letter today. He's arriving by car from Paris. [*Holding up letter*]

MME. DUBONNET

[*Taking the letter*] From Paris, you say?

POLLY

Y-yes. From Paris.

MME. DUBONNET

Then why is this letter postmarked from Nice?

POLLY

Nice? Oh! Oh dear! [*She brings out a hanky*]

MME. DUBONNET

[*Returning the letter*] Do not worry, little Polly. Your secret is safe with me. Voilà! But just tell me one thing.

POLLY

Y-yes, madame?

MME. DUBONNET

How does it happen that one so sweet and charming as you has to pretend to have a—how do you say?—boy friend and write herself love letters?

POLLY

It's because of my father, madame.

MME. DUBONNET

Your father, hein?

POLLY

Yes. You see, when he dies, I shall be really extremely wealthy and he thinks that every man who makes advances to me is just after my fortune.

MME. DUBONNET

So he forbids you to have a boy friend?

POLLY

Well—practically.

MME. DUBONNET

So you invent him?

POLLY

Y-yes, I'm afraid so.

MME. DUBONNET

I see. Poor little rich girl! Well, I too have had a letter today—from your father. He is coming here this morning.

POLLY

Daddy? Coming here?

MME. DUBONNET

Yes. He has been to Toulon on business. When he comes I will have a little word with him.

POLLY

He won't listen.

MME. DUBONNET

Ah, well, we will see. Now dry your eyes and go to your class.

MAISIE ENTERS *through French windows.*

MAISIE

Oh, excusez moi, madame. Je n'avais pas aucune idée que vous êtes ici.

MME. DUBONNET

That is all right, Mademoiselle Merryweather. I was about to go. [*To* POLLY] Soyez gaie, ma petite, and trust in me.

She EXITS.

MAISIE

What was she saying to you, Polly?

POLLY

Oh, nothing. My—my father's coming here today.

MAISIE

Your father? What a thrill! Is he handsome as well as being rich?

POLLY

You wait and see.

She EXITS *laughing.*

MAISIE

Oh, wait for me, Polly! I've left my dorothy bag here some-where. Where on earth can it be?

She starts searching. BOBBY VAN HUSEN APPEARS *at the French windows. He is very good-looking, wears a blazer, flannels and co-respondent shoes. He sees* MAISIE, *creeps in and places his hands over her eyes. She gives a little squeal.*

BOBBY

Guess who?

MAISIE

Bobby! You're crazy to come here! If Madame Dubonnet found out, I would be asked to leave under a cloud!

BOBBY

Oh, she won't find out. I came in the back way.

MAISIE

Well, you must leave at once. Anyone might come in and find us here together.

BOBBY

I'm not leaving here before I make you promise one thing.

MAISIE

Oh, and what is that, may I ask?

BOBBY

Oh, you know as well as I do.

MAISIE

Do I?

BOBBY

Of course you do. I want you to promise to dance every dance at the ball tonight with me.

MAISIE

That's out of the question.

BOBBY

Oh, come on Maisie, be a sport. You know there's no one else I want to dance with but you.

MAISIE

Really? I don't believe it.

BOBBY

Listen baby, to my plea;
Won't you come dancing with me?
Be my baby and say yes.
Or else I'm done for, I guess.

MAISIE

To dance with you is thrilling to
My poor ego.

BOBBY

So, baby, say you're willing to
Shake a leg.
Oh,

Won't you Charleston with me?
Won't you Charleston with me?
And while the band is playing that
Old vodeodo,
Around we will go,
Together we'll show them
How the Charleston is done
We'll surprise everyone.
Just think what Heaven it's going to be
If you will Charleston, Charleston with me.

MAISIE

Won't you Charleston with me?
Won't you Charleston with me?

And while the band is playing that
Old vodeodo,
Around we will go,
Together we'll show them
How the Charleston is done.
We'll surprise everyone.

BOTH

Just think what Heaven it's going to be
If you will Charleston, Charleston with me.

At the end of the dance BOBBY *kisses* MAISIE.

MAISIE

Someone's coming!

BOBBY

I didn't hear anybody.

MAISIE

I did. You must leave at once.

BOBBY

O.K. But don't forget: I'm your dancing partner tonight.

MAISIE

Well, perhaps. I'm not promising anything.

BOBBY

You don't have to. I'm telling you! Good-bye!

MAISIE

Good-bye! Oh, he's gone! Bobby, Bobby, wait for me.

He EXITS *through the French windows. She* EXITS *as* HORTENSE ENTERS *followed by* PERCIVAL BROWNE, *a pompous elderly English gentleman.*

HORTENSE

I will tell Madame Dubonnet you are 'ere, Monsieur Browne. Your hat?

PERCIVAL

Thank you.

She EXITS. PERCIVAL *examines the room.* ENTER MADAME DUBONNET. *On seeing* PERCIVAL *she starts slightly, then controls herself.*

MME. DUBONNET

How do you do, Monsieur Browne. I am Madame Dubonnet.

PERCIVAL

How do you do, Madame. I hope you will forgive this visit at such short notice; but I thought that while I was in the South of France I should visit my daughter's school.

MME. DUBONNET

Quite so, Monsieur. I am so pleased to meet you. We are all so fond of Polly. Asseyez-vous.

PERCIVAL

Ah, yes. A sweet girl. Takes after her poor mother. Wish I could see more of her, but I'm so taken up with business, you know.

MME. DUBONNET

Yes. I understand, Monsieur. But I am sure you would not put it before your daughter's happiness.

PERCIVAL

Polly's happiness? But she's perfectly happy, isn't she? She never complains in her letters.

MME. DUBONNET

Oh, no, I am sure she does not. But there are certain things, Monsieur, which a young girl cannot discuss by post.

PERCIVAL

Oh? Such as what?

MME. DUBONNET

Her heart, Monsieur.

PERCIVAL

Am I to take it, Madame, you are referring to love? I sincerely hope that nothing of that sort is allowed to occur in your school.

MME. DUBONNET

[Laughing] No, no. I do not encourage it on the premises, but—well, les jeunes filles seront les jeunes filles, n'est ce pas?

PERCIVAL

I don't follow you, Madame.

MME. DUBONNET

Surely you have not forgotten all your French, Monsieur Browne—or should I call you mon petit Percy?

PERCIVAL

What! [*Recognising her*] Good heavens! It can't be——!

MME. DUBONNET

Mais oui, mon cher, it is. Do you not remember—your little Kiki!

PERCIVAL

Kiki. This is impossible! Most awkward——!

MME. DUBONNET

But this is no way to greet an old friend! After all we have been to each other? Have you forgotten Armistice night in Maxims, when you——?

PERCIVAL

Yes, Madame, I have. Completely forgotten!

MME. DUBONNET

But surely not, chéri! I wore a red dress, and—you were in uniform. I called you my Tiny Tommy, and we drank champagne. Later on we danced and the orchestra played a waltz which was all the rage in Paris. Let me see, how did it go?

> I still recall so tenderly
> The night when first we met
> The memory's so dear to me,
> So how can you forget?
>
> Fancy forgetting
> The love that we knew
> When we were fancy free.
>
> Fancy forgetting
> What I said to you
> And what you said to me.

PERCIVAL

> Though the years go by
> And our youth is gone,
> Memories don't die,
> Like a song they linger on.

BOTH

> So just when I thought you'd remember it too,
> Fancy, just fancy you forgetting.

At the end of the number, MME. DUBONNET *is about to kiss* PERCIVAL.

PERCIVAL

Kiki! [*Noise of girls, off* L.]

MME. DUBONNET

Ah, the young ladies have finished their classes for the morning. Would you care to accompany me round the school, Monsieur Browne?

PERCIVAL

Yes. Of course, by all means.

MME. DUBONNET

Allons. This way . . . mon petit chou!

PERCIVAL

Oh!

THEY GO OUT. ENTER L. *the* GIRLS *and* POLLY, *laughing and talking.*

DULCIE

Girls, I know. Let's go and try on our costumes before luncheon!

FAY

Yes, let's!

MAISIE

Are you coming too, Polly?

POLLY

Oh, no, I think I'll just stay here. I'm expecting Daddy any moment.

DULCIE

And aren't you expecting *him?*

POLLY

Him? Oh—oh, yes, of course. [GIRLS *giggle*]

MAISIE

Let's leave her, girls. She wants to be alone.

FAY

All right. Bye-bye, Polly!

POLLY

Good-bye!

> *The* GIRLS EXEUNT. *Music.* POLLY *takes out her letter, looks at it sadly, then tears it up. She goes to the window, then turns away with a sob and sits down.* TONY APPEARS *at the window. He wears the uniform of a messenger boy and carries a dress box.*

TONY

[*Coughing*] Er—excusez-moi!

POLLY

[*Turning*] Oh! You startled me!

TONY

I'm sorry, Miss. I'm afraid I came in the wrong way. This is the Villa Caprice, isn't it?

POLLY

Yes.

TONY

Well, I have a package for Miss Polly Browne.

POLLY

Really? How funny!

TONY

Funny? Why?

POLLY

Because I'm Polly Browne.

TONY

Well, it's a very pretty name.

POLLY

Oh, thank you.

TONY

And you live up to it.

POLLY

Oh!

TONY

I'm sorry, Miss. I'm afraid I'm forgetting myself. Here's your package.

POLLY

Oh, thank you.

TONY

If you don't mind my saying so, it's an awfully pretty dress.

POLLY

Yes, it is, isn't it?

TONY

Yes, I'm sure that you—I mean it will be the prettiest at the Ball.

POLLY

Oh, I don't expect so really.

TONY

I do. In fact I know it. I——

POLLY

Yes?

TONY

Well, perhaps I'd better be going.

POLLY

Oh, yes. Oh, no. Oh, yes, perhaps you had. [*He turns to go*] I say!

TONY

[*Turning back*] Yes?

POLLY

You're—you're English, aren't you?

TONY

Yes, as a matter of fact, I am.

POLLY

You don't seem like a messenger boy somehow.

TONY

Don't I? Well, to tell you the truth, I don't usually do this sort of thing, but just at the moment I'm afraid I'm rather on my beam ends.

POLLY

Oh, what a shame! And at Carnival Time too.

TONY

Yes, it is a pity, isn't it? I was hoping I'd be able to go to the Ball tonight. I'll be watching.

POLLY

Will you?

TONY

Of course. [*A pause*]

POLLY

Why don't you come, too?

TONY

Me? Come to the Ball?

POLLY

Yes. Why not? I've got an extra ticket and—oh, dear, you must think me terribly forward.

TONY

No, I don't. I think you're terribly——

POLLY

Yes?

TONY

> I don't claim that I am psychic,
> But one look at you and I kick
> Away every scruple
> I learnt as a pupil
> In school, my dear.

POLLY

> I'm not one to make predictions,
> But I've thrown off all restrictions
> And don't mind confessing
> I think it's a blessing
> That you are here.

TONY

> Though I'm prepared to find I'm wrong,
> I've got a funny feeling we belong
> Together.

I could be happy with you,
If you could be happy with me.

POLLY

I'd be contented to live anywhere,
What would I care,
As long as you were there?

TONY

Skies may not always be blue

POLLY

But one thing is clear as can be

TONY

I know that I could be happy with you,
My darling.

BOTH

If you could be happy with me.

POLLY

Then you will come to the Ball?

TONY

Well, I'll try. I'll have to see about a costume.

POLLY

There's a Pierrot's costume at Gaston's. Couldn't you borrow it?

TONY

Well, I'll see. How can I let you know?

POLLY

Let me think. I'll be on the Plage at three o'clock this afternoon—beside the bandstand.

TONY

Three o'clock, beside the bandstand. Good-bye till then!

POLLY

Good-bye! [*He* EXITS] And I don't even know his name.

RE-ENTER MADAME DUBONNET *and* PERCIVAL. *Simultaneously the* GIRLS *drift on.*

MME. DUBONNET

Polly, I have a visitor for you!

POLLY

Oh, Daddy! [*She runs to him*] I'm so happy!

PERCIVAL

Are you, my dear? I'm very glad to hear it!

MAISIE

Has he arrived yet, Polly?

POLLY

Yes, he's arrived! He's really arrived!

Ensemble—THE BOY FRIEND.

CURTAIN

ACT TWO

ACT TWO

¶ *The Plage. The same afternoon. The sea is in the background. Downstage is the promenade.*

As the curtain rises the GIRLS *and the* BOYS *are on . . . the* GIRLS *wear bathing costumes, the* BOYS *white flannels.*

BOYS and GIRLS

What a lovely day
What a lovely day
For a dip in the sea.
Oh, what fun it will be!
Won't you come and have a swim with me?

DULCIE

But whatever you do
When I'm swimming with you,
Please remember not to go too far.

BOYS

Though you may look cute
In your bathing suit,
We don't know who you are.

BOYS and GIRLS

There's no knowing
Who you are going
To meet sur le Plage.

DULCIE

You may run up against a rajah,

NANCY

Or maybe your man

DULCIE

Will be a poor man.

BOYS and GIRLS

Sal or Susie
Cannot be choosey,
For here love's a guessing game.

GIRLS

Sur le Plage.

BOYS

Sur le Plage.

BOYS and GIRLS

Everyone looks the same.

There's no saying
Who may be playing
With you sur le Plage.

BOYS

A knight who's left behind his charger

NANCY

May call you ducky.

DULCIE

Won't you be lucky?

BOYS and GIRLS

In the ocean
You'll find emotion
May play you a funny game
Sur le Plage,
Sur le Plage,
Everyone looks the same.

ENTER LORD BROCKHURST R., *a jolly English aristocrat with a monocle and high blood pressure. He has his eye on the* GIRLS.

ALPHONSE

Dulcie, come along, Dulcie! Come and swim with us.

The BOYS *and* GIRLS EXEUNT, LADY BROCKHURST ENTERS, *gaunt and severe, with parasol.*

LADY B.

Hubert! Hubert! Where are you?

LORD B.

Oh—er—here, my dear. Just admiring the view!

LADY B.

So I see. So different from Bognor, isn't it?

LORD B.

Oh, yes, indeed! Much prettier!

LADY B.

I'm not so sure about that, Hubert. I'm beginning to think we should have gone there in the first place.

LORD B.

Nonsense, Hilda! Nothing like a change from routine for old people like us, I feel twenty years younger.

LADY B.

And behaving accordingly, I notice. Really, Hubert, how can you, after our loss. [*She brings out hanky*]

LORD B.

Now, now, Hilda, don't take on so. After all, Tony isn't dead, is he?

LADY B.

He might as well be. Sometimes when I think of the disgrace, I would rather he were.

LORD B.

Oh, come now! After all, the boy has done nothing wrong.

LADY B.

Nothing wrong? Disappearing from Oxford in the middle of Hilary term, ruining a brilliant career! Why, they won't even consider him for the constituency now!

ENTER DULCIE, NANCY *and* FAY.

LORD B.

Well, never mind, dear. Perhaps he's found another career.

LADY B.

But he hasn't any money, Hubert! Not a penny to his name. Oh, dear, it gives me palpitations every time I think of it. I shall have to go and sit in a shelter.

LORD B.

[*Ogling the girls*] Very well, my dear.

LADY B.

Hubert!

LORD B.

Oh—er—yes, dear.

They GO OUT. GIRLS *giggle.*

DULCIE

Well, who's for a dip?

FAY

I am; are you coming, Maisie?

MAISIE

[ENTERING] Righto! How about you, Polly?

POLLY

[ENTERING] Oh, no, I think I'll just have a stroll.

DULCIE

Are you meeting *him?*

POLLY

Yes, as a matter of fact I am!

FAY

Oh, please may we stay and meet him too?

MAISIE

Don't be a ninny, Fay. Polly doesn't want us around. [GIRLS *giggle*]

OMNES

See you later, Polly.

DULCIE

Come along, Nancy.

They wave to her and GO OFF. POLLY *wanders up and down looking a little anxious and glancing at her wrist-watch.* TONY ENTERS L. *He now wears a blazer and flannels. He coughs.*

POLLY

Oh! There you are!

TONY

Yes. Did you think I wasn't coming?

POLLY

Well, I—wasn't sure.

TONY

Well, you ought to have been. And I've seen Monsieur Gaston about a costume and it's all right.

POLLY

Now I shall really enjoy the Carnival Ball.

TONY

So shall I! By Jove, I never thought I should be going to it with anyone like you. It makes me feel rather nervous.

POLLY

Nervous? Why?

TONY

Well, me just a messenger boy and you a rich young lady from the Villa Caprice.

POLLY

Rich? Oh, I'm not rich. You see—I just work there as Madame
Dubonnet's secretary.

TONY

Do you honestly? Then we're not so different after all.

POLLY

No.

TONY

I'm so glad. I thought you would only like the grand life—you
know, big cars, diamonds and champagne.

POLLY

Oh, no. I'm quite content with simple things.

TONY

How ripping. So am I . . .

A life of wealth does not appeal to me at all
Do you agree at all?

POLLY

I do.

TONY

The mere idea of living in a palace is
So full of fallacies.

POLLY

That's true.

TONY

I've got a very different sort of scheme in mind,
It's just a dream designed
For two.
Would you care to hear about it, dear?

POLLY

Would I care to? Can you doubt it, dear?

TONY

All I want is a room
In Bloomsbury,
Just a room that will do
For you and me.
One room's enough for us,
Though it's on the top floor.
Life may be rough for us,
But its troubles we'll ignore.
On a wintery night
I'll light a fire.
Everything I shall do
As you desire.

POLLY

You'll be sitting,

TONY

And you'll be knitting,
And so contented we'll be
In our dear little room in Bloomsbury.

POLLY

All we want is a room
In Bloomsbury,
Just a room that will do
For you and me.
I'll sew the covers for
Two old cosy armchairs.
Neighbours will love us for
We shall laugh at all our cares.

TONY

While I'm reading a book

POLLY

I'll cook a stew.
Then I'll bake a plum duff
Enough for two.

BOTH

In our attic
We'll be ecstatic
As lovebirds up in a tree.
All we want is a room in Bloomsbury.

TONY

Wouldn't it be wonderful?

At the end of the number TONY *and* POLLY *are about to kiss.*
ENTER HORTENSE *wearing her Sunday best. She gives a gasp
of surprise on seeing* POLLY. POLLY *turns round and sees
her.*

HORTENSE

Oh, Mam'selle Browne!

POLLY

Hortense!

HORTENSE

What would Madame Dubonnet say if she saw you kissing a young man in public?

POLLY

Oh, please don't tell her, Hortense!

TONY

Dash it all, I don't see why she should care what you do on your afternoon off.

HORTENSE

One does not take the afternoon off from being a perfect young lady, Monsieur. [*Recognising him*] Oh, mon dieu!

POLLY

What is the matter, Hortense?

HORTENSE

Do you know who he is? He is just a messenger boy from Gaston's.

POLLY

Well, yes, I know. But he's awfully nice——

HORTENSE

If Madame Dubonnet knew that one of her young ladies——

POLLY

Please, Hortense! Let me talk to you.

TONY

Well, shall I go?

POLLY

Oh, no, Tony. I won't be a minute.

She comes downstage with HORTENSE.

POLLY

Dear Hortense, don't betray me. I know he is just a messenger boy; but he is doing it because he is poor, and I'm sure that in reality he is as well born as I am.

HORTENSE

Perhaps so. But he has no right to make advances to a young lady like yourself in his present condition.

POLLY

But—he thinks I'm just a secretary.

HORTENSE

You told him that?

POLLY

Y-yes, I did.

HORTENSE

Hélas, quelle situation!

POLLY

Please, Hortense, don't let on to anyone. I am so happy to have an admirer who isn't just interested in my wealth. Surely you must know how I feel?

HORTENSE

[*Softening*] Perhaps I do. But if Madame Dubonnet should find out——

POLLY

Oh, she won't. That is unless *you* tell her.

HORTENSE

All right, ma petite, I give you my promise. After all, it is Carnival Time.

POLLY

Thank you, Hortense! I shan't forget.

[*Sounds of laughter off*]

HORTENSE

Oh, here come the other young ladies.

POLLY

Oh, dear! Let's go, Tony. I don't want to meet them just now. They do chatter so.

TONY

All right, Polly. Let's nip over to the promenade.

POLLY

Good-bye, Hortense! And don't forget—ssh! You promised!

HORTENSE *waves to her.* ENTER DULCIE, FAY, MARCEL, PIERRE *and others as required.* EXEUNT POLLY *and* TONY.

DULCIE

I say, wasn't that Polly?

FAY

I'm sure it was. I recognised her frock.

DULCIE

Oh, look, there's Hortense! Hortense, do tell us, was that Mademoiselle Browne with her beau?

HORTENSE

I have no idea.

FAY

Oh, yes, you have. Go on, Hortense, do tell!

OMNES

Yes, do tell. [*Etc.*]

DULCIE

Is he terribly slick and handsome?

HORTENSE

I do not know what you are talking about.

FAY

Oh, isn't she mean? If you just tell me what he's like, Hortense, I'll give you that handkerchief sachet.

DULCIE

And I'll give you those crocheted flowers.

HORTENSE

Taisez-vous, mademoiselles! It is not seemly to be so curious about a young man.

FAY

And why not? Haven't you ever been curious, Hortense?

HORTENSE

Well, I—

MARCEL

Mais oui, Hortense, I believe you have.

HORTENSE

Zut!

PIERRE

Hortense is not so prim as she pretends, eh?

HORTENSE

Oh, la la!

DULCIE, FAY and NANCY

Of course she isn't! After all, she *is* French!

HORTENSE

Yes, I am. And I am very proud of it, too.

> I'm often asked if I would like to travel
> And visit other lands across the sea
> But though it might be pleasant,
> I think that for the present,
> This is the place that I prefer to be.
> Let others go to Sweden or Siam,
> I think I'll stay exactly where I am.

They say it's lovely when a
Young lady's in Vienna,
But it's nicer, much nicer in Nice.
In Amsterdam or Brussels
The men have great big muscles,
But they're nicer, much nicer in Nice.
I've heard that the Italians
Are very fond of dalliance,
And they're also keen on it in Greece.
But whatever they may say,
This is where I want to stay,
For it's so much nicer in Nice.

BOYS and GIRLS

She says it's nicer, much nicer in Nice
She says it's nicer, much nicer in Nice.

HORTENSE

Some people's one desire is
To go to Buenos Aires,
But it's nicer, much nicer in Nice.
The laws are rather vague in
The town of Copenhagen,
But they're nicer, much nicer in Nice.
And some may like a flutter
In Bombay or Calcutta,
But they might have trouble with the police (Oh, la, la!)
Other places may be fun,
But when all is said and done,
It is so much nicer in Nice.

The number ends with HORTENSE *in a daring attitude supported by the* BOYS.

MARCEL

Prenez garde—Madame Dubonnet!

HORTENSE

Oh, here comes Madame Dubonnet! If she finds me like this,
I shall get the—bag!

DULCIE

She means the sack!

FAY

Come along, Nancy.

EXEUNT OMNES. ENTER MADAME DUBONNET *and* PERCIVAL.

MME. DUBONNET

This way, mon petit chou. The water will be as warm as toast.

PERCIVAL

Er—on second thoughts, madame——

MME. DUBONNET

Why do you not call me Kiki as you used to in the old days?

PERCIVAL

All right, Kiki. But I don't think I want to bathe, after all.

MME. DUBONNET

But why not, chéri? It will do you good.

PERCIVAL

I can't swim.

ENTER LORD B. *backwards.*

MME. DUBONNET

Aha, I think you are telling a little fib—yes? I'm sure you can swim just like a fish—with all these big muscles. [*Pinching him*]

PERCIVAL

Oh! Kiki, don't! I'm ticklish!

MME. DUBONNET

I know. I remember! [LORD B. *is fascinated*]

PERCIVAL

Someone will see!

MME. DUBONNET

Who cares? This is the Riviera! Now come along, we are going
to have our bathe.

PERCIVAL

But—but I haven't brought a bathing costume!

MME. DUBONNET

Ça n'fait rien!

PERCIVAL

You don't mean I should bathe without——

MME. DUBONNET

Non, non! But I know where I can borrow one for you. So you
wait here, I will return dans un instant.

PERCIVAL

But, Kiki——

MME. DUBONNET

Au revoir, mon petit poisson! [EXIT *laughing*]

PERCIVAL

Kiki!

PERCY *makes as if to follow her, decides against it. He
turns back.*

LORD B.

Psst! I say! [PERCY *takes no notice*] I say, old chap!

PERCIVAL

Were you addressing me?

LORD B.

Well, I wasn't addressing the chair! Actually, old boy, I was wondering if you could help me. You seem to know your way about here—all the jolliest girls. I'm a stranger here, you see, and what's more—[*whispers*]—I've got the wife in tow. She's not a bad sort really, but—*she doesn't understand me.*

PERCIVAL

I'm afraid I can't assist you in your domestic affairs.

LORD B.

I don't want assistance in my domestic affairs. It's *foreign* affairs I'm talking about! Now, come on, old chap, we Englishmen abroad must stick together, you know.

PERCIVAL

Yes, of course.

LORD B.

Now what about this little lady you were dallying with just now? She seems a sporty little filly!

PERCIVAL

Sporty little filly! Really, sir, I must ask you to control your language. That lady is a highly esteemed member of the community.

LORD B.

Oh, yes yes, I'm sure she is. They manage these things so much better in France.

PERCIVAL

She is, sir, a headmistress.

LORD B.

I say! You are in luck, aren't you?

PERCIVAL

[*Disgusted*] Oh! [RE-ENTER MADAME DUBONNET]

LORD B.

Ah, here she comes! Now be a good fellow and introduce us.

MME. DUBONNET

[*Holding up a large striped bathing costume*] Look, Percy, the latest model!

PERCIVAL

I'm sorry, Madame. I have changed my mind, I'm going straight back to my hotel.

MME. DUBONNET

But Percy, I have got you such a lovely costume. You mustn't disappoint me now.

LORD B.

Go on, old chap, do as she says. [*Raises hat to* MADAME DUBONNET *who bridles*]

PERCIVAL

I've had enough of this, I'm leaving at once.

MME. DUBONNET

Are you, Percy? What have I done?

LORD B.

I say, old chap, you're upsetting her. You know that's no way to treat a headmistress! [*Laughter*]

PERCIVAL

Will you please go away?

MME. DUBONNET

But Percy, will you not introduce me to your friend? Perhaps he would like to come bathing instead, hein?

LORD B.

[*Galvanised*] By Jove, like a shot!

PERCIVAL

Kiki, this gentleman is a complete stranger to me. I've never met him before in my life.

LORD B.

But this is France, my good man. We can afford to dispenser avec les formalités, n'est ce pas? [*To* MADAME DUBONNET]

MME. DUBONNET

Mais oui, Monsieur, vous avez raison!

LORD B.

I don't know what that means, but it sounds absolutely delicious.

PERCIVAL

Oh!

ENTER LADY B.

LADY B.

Hubert! Where have you disappeared to now?

LORD B.

Botheration!

LADY B.

[*Seeing him*] Hubert! Come here at once!

LORD B.

Very well, my dear. I was just asking this lady and gentleman the way to the—er——

LADY B.

Hubert! Remember we are British.

EXEUNT LORD AND LADY B.

MME. DUBONNET

[*Laughing*] Oh, le pauvre petit homme!

PERCIVAL

Really, what an embarrassing situation!

MME. DUBONNET

Aha, Percy, I think you were a little jealous, no?

PERCIVAL

Not at all. I just like people to behave decently, that's all.

MME. DUBONNET

Just as we were beginning to enjoy ourselves!

PERCIVAL

I must have been out of my mind.

MME. DUBONNET

Oh, you are what you call a—damp blanket. You spoil all the fun.

PERCIVAL

It's high time you realised that things are very different from what they were.

MME. DUBONNET

Are they, Percy? [*Vamping him*]

PERCIVAL

Yes, most definitely.

MME. DUBONNET

Percy, Percy,
Please have mercy.
Why must you always be so sad and gloomy?
Why can't you be a little nicer to me?
Chéri, chéri,
Please be merry.
When I am trying to be bright and jolly,
It isn't nice to be so melancholy.

Oh, dear,
I've got the you-don't-want-to-play-with-me blues.

PERCIVAL

Don't-want-to-play-with-me blues.

MME. DUBONNET

It's clear
I've got the you-don't-want-to-stay-with-me blues.

PERCIVAL

Don't-want-to-stay-with-me blues.

MME. DUBONNET

I am so good
At spreading mirth and joy.
But it's no good
With such a sulky boy.

I try
To play the game the other fellows all choose.

PERCIVAL

The other fellows all choose.

MME. DUBONNET

I sigh
Because you always refuse.
What is a girl to do
With such a boy as you?
I've got those
Dreary
Weary
You-don't-want-to-play-with-me blues.

At the end of the number all EXEUNT. ENTER MAISIE L. *and*
BOBBY R.

BOBBY

Maisie! Maisie! Here you are at last! I've been looking every-where for you.

MAISIE

Have you? I've been for a swim with Dulcie and Fay.

BOBBY

Just Dulcie and Fay? Are you sure there wasn't anyone else with you?

MAISIE

What if there was? I can go bathing with whom I choose.

BOBBY

I wish you'd choose me.

MAISIE

I don't want to choose anyone in particular.

ENTER BOYS.

BOBBY

Why not?

MAISIE

Because I want to have a good time whilst I'm young. After all, I'm only seventeen . . .

BOBBY

But I can give you a good time. It's not as if I hadn't got plenty of cash.

MAISIE

Money isn't everything.

BOBBY

When are you going to come and see my yacht again? You liked that, didn't you?

MAISIE

Oh yes, it's a very dinky yacht. [*Waving to* MARCEL] Hullo, Marcel!

MARCEL

Mam'selle Maisie! You look ravissante! Don't forget you promised to dance the tango with me tonight.

MAISIE

Of course not!

BOBBY

But Maisie——!

MAISIE

Oh, Pierre!

PIERRE

Mam'selle Maisie! You look enchanting. Tonight you and I will dance the two-step, yes?

MAISIE

I can hardly wait.

BOBBY

Hey, Maisie——!

MAISIE

Alphonse!

ALPHONSE

I too want to dance with you at the Ball.

MAISIE

And so you shall!

BOBBY

Maisie! Listen to me!

BOYS

Listen to all of us!

BOBBY

You're so fascinating

MARCEL

But it's aggravating

PIERRE

That you keep us waiting
To hear

ALPHONSE

Which one will be

BOYS

Your favourite he.

MARCEL

You're so very taking

PIERRE

That our hearts are breaking

BOBBY

So you should be making
It clear

BOYS

Which one of us
You rate alpha plus.

MAISIE

Now listen, boys, you should recall
I've often said I love you all.

BOYS

You love us all?

MAISIE

Yes, I love you all.
It's time you learned
That I am no fool.
Where love's concerned
I stick to this rule.

There's safety in numbers,
That's what I believe.
The girl who knows
A lot of beaux
Is never likely to grieve.
The lady who slumbers
Is left high and dry.
But I'm awake
And never miss

The chance to take
Another kiss.
There's safety in numbers
And the more the merrier am I.

At the end of it they ALL GO OFF. RE-ENTER POLLY *and*
TONY.

TONY

All right, Polly, the coast's clear!

POLLY

I think perhaps I'd better be getting back to the Villa. I have some letters to type.

TONY

Oh, do you have to go so soon?

POLLY

Yes, I'm afraid I must. But I'll see you at the Ball tonight, won't I?

TONY

I should jolly well think so. Where shall I meet you?

POLLY

I don't know. You say.

TONY

Well, how about the Café Pataplon at nine o'clock?

POLLY

Lovely! I shall be waiting for you.

TONY

Tonight seems a very long time away.

POLLY

It's not really. Only a few hours.

TONY

Yes, and it's going to be a wonderful evening, isn't it—Polly?

POLLY

I'm sure it is—Tony.

TONY

But it's just the first of lots of wonderful evenings—isn't it?

POLLY

Yes—at least—I expect so.

TONY

But why shouldn't it be? Remember what you said this morning?

POLLY

What did I say?

TONY

I could be so happy with you,
If you could be happy with me.

POLLY

I'd be contented to live anywhere.
What would I care,
As long as you were there?

TONY

Skies may not always be blue,
But one thing is clear as can be,

BOTH

I know that I could be happy with you,
My darling,
If you could be happy with . . .

POLLY

Oh, Tony! And now I really must go.

ENTER LORD *and* LADY B.

TONY

[*Taking her hand*] Polly.

POLLY

Yes?

TONY

Will you—would you—kiss me good-bye?

POLLY

Yes, if you want me to.

He kisses her. LORD *and* LADY B. *see* TONY. LADY B. *shows
agitation.* TONY *sees them. Crowd begin to drift on.*

TONY

Oh, gosh!

POLLY

What's the matter?

TONY

I—I've got to hop it, Polly—quickly!

LADY B.

I tell you it *was* he, Hubert! I saw him quite distinctly.

ENTER GENDARME.

LORD B.

Are you sure, dear?

POLLY

But—but why must you go?

TONY

I can't explain now. I'll—I'll see you tonight.

POLLY

But—but—oh, dear.

LORD B.

Then we must call the police. Hey, you there! Gendarme! Gendarme!

EXIT TONY, *followed by* GENDARME

LADY B.

Gendarme! Gendarme! Stop that man!

POLLY

Calling the police! Oh, surely not! [*To* MARCEL] Oh, Marcel, tell me quickly, who are that lady and gentleman?

MARCEL

It is the rich milor Brockhurst and his wife. They seem to be chasing a thief.

POLLY

[*In soliloquy*] A thief! Oh, no, it couldn't be. And yet they are rich. And he is penniless, he told me so himself—oh, dear, he must have known all along that I am not a working girl but a millionaire's daughter. Oh, dear! He's just like all the rest. [*She breaks down*]

DULCIE

[*Running over to her*] Polly? Did he steal something from you too?

POLLY

Yes, Dulcie, he did.

DULCIE

Not your gold bangle?

POLLY

Not my gold bangle. Something much more precious.

MME. DUBONNET

[*Coming to* POLLY] What is the matter, ma petite? You look quite pale.

HORTENSE

[*Joining them*] I think I can explain, Madame. That man was Monsieur . . .

No, Hortense! You promised!

MME. DUBONNET

But what is it, Polly?

POLLY

It's nothing, Madame. I'm just a little disappointed, that's all.
You see, I shan't be going to the Carnival Ball after all . . .

I could be happy with you,
If you could be happy with me.
I'd be contented to live anywhere.
What would I care,
As long as you were there?

ALL

Skies may not always be blue,
But one thing is clear as can be,
I know that I could be happy with you,
My darling,
If you could be happy with me.

POLLY *runs off in tears.*

C U R T A I N

ACT THREE

ACT THREE

¶ *The Terrasse of the Café Pataplon. That night.*

The BOYS *and* GIRLS *are dancing.* LORD B. *is staggering around. They drink, laugh and chatter.* ENTER HORTENSE *in peasant costume.*

MARCEL

Voilà la belle Hortense!

DULCIE

I say, girls, doesn't Hortense look a picture?

They gather round her.

BOBBY

How many hearts are you going to break tonight, Hortense?

HORTENSE

Taisez-vous, mon petit gars! There are ladies present.

MAISIE

Oh, don't be so prim, Hortense! You know you'll soon be as tiddly as all the rest of us!

FAY

I must say your get-up is terribly natty!

HORTENSE

It is just an old peasant frock belonging to ma mère.

DULCIE

Hortense, do tell us. Did you see Polly before you left? Is she still determined not to come to the Ball?

HORTENSE

I'm afraid so. I tried to persuade her to come with me, but she said she wished to go to bed.

MAISIE

Oh, what a frost! Now we shall never know who her boy friend is.

ENTER MADAME DUBONNET *and* PERCIVAL.

PIERRE

Regardez! Regardez! C'est le père de Polly avec Madame Dubonnet.

LORD B.

Dubonnet? That's a familiar word! [EXIT]

MAISIE

Oh, doesn't she look lovely.

MADAME DUBONNET *and* PERCIVAL *come down* C. *The others* EXEUNT.

MME. DUBONNET

Are you not glad you came to the Ball after all?

PERCIVAL

I'm not a bit glad. I feel such a fool in this costume.

MME. DUBONNET

You look ravissant, mon cher—formidable! Have some champagne and then you will feel more like enjoying yourself.

PERCIVAL

I'd feel happier if I knew how Polly is. She seemed so miserable this afternoon.

MME. DUBONNET

She is in love, pauvre petite!

PERCIVAL

In love? Do you honestly believe that?

MME. DUBONNET

Yes, mon vieux, I do. It takes a woman to understand these things.

PERCIVAL

I'm beginning to believe you're right. Perhaps Polly misses her mother more than I realised.

MME. DUBONNET

Every girl needs a mother when she is young.

PERCIVAL

I have been selfish, Kiki. I have neglected Polly. When she needed comfort, I was far away. So she turned instead to you. For that I shall always be grateful.

MME. DUBONNET

It was nothing. You know, sometimes I feel as if little Polly were like my own daughter.

PERCIVAL

She could be, Kiki, she could be——

MME. DUBONNET

What did you say, chéri?

PERCIVAL

I was a fool to pretend the old Percy was dead. Ah, Kiki, you are still as beautiful as ever! It seems as though time has stood still and we are once more dancing in that tiny café in Montparnasse at three o'clock in the morning.

They dance.

MME. DUBONNET

Do you remember the dear old waiter with the red nose?

PERCIVAL

And the fat lady behind the counter who went to sleep and snored?

MME. DUBONNET

And you said—you said you wanted the night to go on for ever!

PERCIVAL

Kiki, give me that champagne.

MME. DUBONNET

So—you are beginning to remember.

PERCIVAL

Yes, Kiki, I am beginning to remember.

They EXEUNT.

BOBBY *and* MAISIE RUN ON.

MAISIE

Let's sit down, Bobby. I'm exhausted.

BOBBY

But it's early yet. I thought you said you were going to dance all night.

MAISIE

Yes, I know I did. But I'm worried about Polly. I made her promise to come to the Ball, but Hortense said she was going to bed. It does seem a shame.

BOBBY

Maybe it is. But don't worry about her. I'm the one you've got to worry about from now on.

MAISIE

Oh? And why, may I ask?

BOBBY

Because—because I want you to marry me, baby.

MAISIE

Marry you? Oh, Bobby, do you really mean it?

BOBBY

Of course I do. Will you, Maisie?

MAISIE

I don't know. You must give me time to think.

BOBBY

Well, how much time?

MAISIE

Until—until midnight tonight. I'll let you know then. I promise.

BOBBY

Okay, baby, but I sure hope the answer is yes.

ENTER DULCIE, ALPHONSE, PIERRE, NANCY, MARCEL *and* FAY *in state of excitement.*

DULCIE

Oh, there you are, Maisie! We've been looking for you everywhere.

FAY

You must come and talk to us. We've got the most tremendous news.

MAISIE

[*Joining them*] So have I.

BOBBY

But Maisie! What about our dance?

MAISIE

It'll have to wait. I've got to chat to my chums.

The GIRLS *are downstage* R. *The* BOYS *gather downstage* L.

DULCIE

Maisie, you'll never guess what's happened to us. We've been proposed to!

MAISIE

What a coincidence! So have I!

DULCIE

By Bobby van Husen? [MAISIE *nods*]

FAY

Are you going to accept him?

MAISIE

I don't know yet. I want to keep him on a string.

DULCIE

Silly Maisie.

MAISIE

Who proposed to you?

DULCIE

Alphonse!

NANCY

Pierre!

FAY

Marcel! And we haven't accepted them yet, either.

ALL

Poor boys! We've got them all on tenterhooks.

MAISIE

I told Bobby I'd let him know at midnight.

DULCIE

What a splendid notion! I say, girls, let's do the same.

FAY

Rightiho!

DULCIE

Alphonse!

ALPHONSE

Oui.

FAY

Marcel!

MARCEL

Oui.

NANCY

Pierre!

PIERRE

Oui.

DULCIE, FAY and NANCY

Thank you very much for your proposal. We'll let you know at midnight.

MARCEL

At midnight? But it is so long to wait.

PIERRE

They are just torturing us, ces jeunes filles.

BOBBY

I know. And it's not fair. Maisie, you planned this.

MAISIE

Well, you'll just have to put up with it, won't they, girls?

DULCIE, FAY and NANCY

Yes!

BOBBY

Okay, so we will. But at least we can make the time pass quickly.

MARCEL, PIERRE and ALPHONSE

How?

BOBBY

We can dance.

ALL

Yes!

BOBBY and MAISIE

When trouble troubles you,
The only thing to do
Is dance, you simply gotta dance.

BOYS and GIRLS

And if you've had a tiff,
You'll soon forget it, if
You dance, you simply gotta dance.
Here in the South of France
They've got a new step.
It's quite the cutest dance
Invented to step
So do step.

GIRLS

Wriggle your hips and kick up your heels,
You'll be surprised how lovely it feels.

BOYS and GIRLS

Everybody's doing the Riviera.

BOYS

Wiggle your fingers, waggle your toes,
Just how it started nobody knows.

BOYS and GIRLS

Everybody's doing the Riviera.

Multi-millionaires and their little pets
Do it.
Even maiden ladies who wear lorgnettes
Have taken to it.

Tell everyone to give out the news.
This is the way to shake off the blues.
Everybody's doing the Riviera.

Get on the dance floor, get in the swing,
This is the time for having a fling.
Everybody's doing the Riviera.

❋　　❋　　❋

Clap-a your hand and slap on your thighs,
Grin like a goon and roll up your eyes,
Everybody's doing the Riviera.

BOYS and GIRLS

All the bright young things and their bright
Young beaux
Do it.
Even duchesses and their gigolos
Have taken to it.

Ain't it terrific? Ain't it the top?
You gotta dance right on till you drop.
Everybody's doing the Riviera.

At the end of the dance they all go OFF. ENTER HORTENSE.

HORTENSE

Oh! Champagne!

ENTER TONY *with parcel.* MUSIC

HORTENSE

Oh! It is you.

TONY

Oh! [*He makes as if to go off*]

HORTENSE

Attendez! Attendez! I wish to have a word with you!

TONY

But I'm in a great hurry.

HORTENSE

You were in a great hurry this afternoon too, n'est ce pas? Leaving poor Miss Polly without a word! Ah, les hommes, les hommes.

TONY

Er—how is Polly?

HORTENSE

Broken-hearted, pauvre petite. She refuses to come to the Ball, even though I did my best to persuade her.

TONY

Does she—does she want to see me?

HORTENSE

Who knows? But it is a pity she is not here enjoying herself in her pretty costume.

TONY

Yes, it was pretty, wasn't it?

HORTENSE

But of course if she has no partner to dance with, she might just as well stay at home.

TONY

[*Looking at the parcel*] I wonder if—but I don't suppose she wants to speak to me. She probably thinks I'm just a common philanderer. [HORTENSE *says nothing*] And yet, if you could persuade her to come to the Ball, I know I could prove that I really love her.

HORTENSE

Well, I do not know if that would be the right thing to do. But——

TONY

Yes——?

HORTENSE

I think perhaps, in spite of all, she loves you too.

TONY

Do you honestly?

HORTENSE

So if you promise not to run away——

TONY

Oh, I do, Hortense. And merci beaucoup! Well, I'll go and

change into my costume. I was just going to take it back to Gaston's, but, thank goodness, I ran into you.

HORTENSE

Do not thank me yet, mon vieux. She may not come at all. [EXIT]

> TONY *dances with box and* EXIT. ENTER BOYS *and* GIRLS, *followed by* LORD B. *Laughter and gaiety in the course of which* DULCIE *slaps* PIERRE'S *face.* EXEUNT OMNES, *leaving* DULCIE *disgruntled.* LORD B. *sees* DULCIE *and approaches her.*

LORD B.

Er—bonsoir, ma petite!

DULCIE

Oh! You startled me!

LORD B.

Ah, you're English. I thought you were French.

DULCIE

Oh, did you honestly? Well, I'm not.

LORD B.

I didn't mean to be rude.

DULCIE

Oh, that's all right. It's just that I'm rather fed-up with France.

LORD B.

Are you? I can't imagine how a pretty girl like you could be fed-up with anything.

DULCIE

Well, I am. And not just with France. I'm also fed-up with boys.

LORD B.

With boys? Well, then, why not try something older?

DULCIE

Something older?

LORD B.

Yes, like me for instance.

LORD B.

I may be too old to run a mile.

DULCIE

Run a mile?

LORD B.

Yes, run a mile.
But there's one thing I still do very well.
I may be too old to climb a stile.

DULCIE

Climb a stile?

LORD B.

Yes, climb a stile.
But there's one thing at which I still excel.
Although my hair is turning grey,

DULCIE

Yes, it's rather grey.

LORD B.

I still believe it when I say.

DULCIE

Well, what do you say?

LORD B.

It's never too late to have a fling
For autumn is just as nice as spring,
And it's never too late to fall in love.

DULCIE

Boop a Doop, Boop a Doop, Boop a Doop.

LORD B.

It's never too late to wink an eye,
I'll do it until the day I die,
And it's never too late to fall in love.

DULCIE

Boop a Doop, Boop a Doop, Boop a Doop.

LORD B.

If they say I'm too old for you,

DULCIE

Then I shall answer 'Why, sir,
One never drinks the wine that's new;
The old wine tastes much nicer.'

LORD B.

A gentleman never feels too weak
To pat a pink arm or pinch a cheek,
And it's never too late to fall in love.

DULCIE

Sez who?

LORD B.

Sez me.

DULCIE

Sez you.

LORD B.

Sez we.

BOTH

Sez both of us together.

LORD B.

It's never too late to whisper words

DULCIE

Concerning the ways of bees and birds,

LORD B.

And it's never too late

DULCIE

To fall in love.

BOYS and GIRLS

Whack a Do, Whack a Do, Whack a Do.

DULCIE

It's never too late to flirt and spoon,

LORD B.

A fiddle that's old is more in tune,

DULCIE

And it's never too late

LORD B.

To fall in love.

BOYS and GIRLS

Whack a Do, Whack a Do, Whack a Do.

DULCIE

The modern artists of today
May paint their pictures faster.
But when it comes to skill, I say—

LORD B.

You can't beat an old master.

It's never too late to bill and coo,

DULCIE

At any age one and one make two,

LORD B.

And it's never too late to fall in

DULCIE

Never too late to fall in

LORD B.

Never too late to fall in

DULCIE

Love.

     ✿   ✿   ✿

It's never too late to blow a kiss
Especially at a time like this

LORD B.

And it's never too late to fall in love.

DULCIE

Vodeo, vodeo, vodeo.

LORD B.

It's never too late for fun and larks,
A jolly old flame has lots of sparks,

DULCIE

And it's never too late to fall in love.

LORD B.

Vodeo, vodeo, vodeo.

DULCIE

The modern buildings that you see
Are often most alarming.

LORD B.

But I am sure that you'll agree

DULCIE

A ruin

LORD B.

Can be charming.

DULCIE

It's never too late to be a beau,

LORD B.

Experience counts a lot, you know,

BOTH

And it's never too late to fall in
Never too late to fall in
Never too late to fall in love.

As it ends, LADY B. ENTERS. *She sees* LORD B. *and* DULCIE.

LADY B.

Hubert!

LORD B.

Oh, lord, the wife! [*To* DULCIE] Run along now, there's a good girl.

DULCIE *laughs. She blows him a kiss and* RUNS OFF.

LADY B.

And who, may I ask, was that?

LORD B.

Oh—er—just an acquaintance, my dear; we were merely passing the time of day.

LADY B.

What, at this time of night? Really, Hubert, you are disgraceful!

LORD B.

Disgraceful? But I wasn't misbehaving.

LADY B.

I'm not so sure. In any case I can't think why you should wish to attend this wicked Ball, when you know how distressed I am. Our experience this afternoon has quite unnerved me.

LORD B.

Now, now, Hilda, don't take on so. Come and sit down and I'll ask the garçon to bring a glass of port.

LADY B.

I don't require anything to drink, thank you, Hubert. I intend to return to the hotel in a few minutes, and I shall expect you to accompany me.

LORD B.

Very well, my dear. Just as you wish. Garçon, garçon, bring the lady a glass of port.

The BOYS *and* GIRLS, MADAME DUBONNET *and* PERCIVAL ENTER.

MAISIE

Oh, look, everybody, here comes Polly!

ENTER POLLY. *She is dressed as Pierrette and looks disconsolate.*

PERCIVAL

So she's come to the Ball after all. Poor child, how sad she looks.

MME. DUBONNET

Let me talk to her, mon vieux. I know how she is feeling.

She goes up to POLLY *and leads her to a table.*

LADY B.

Hubert, I think that's the girl we saw with Tony this afternoon.

LORD B.

Are you sure?

LADY B.

Positive. Perhaps if we talked to her, she might be able to tell us his whereabouts.

LORD B.

Yes. I'll have a word with her in a minute.

LADY B.

No, Hubert. We'll both have a word with her, later.

MME. DUBONNET

[*To* POLLY] Polly, you look charming.

POLLY

Do I, Madame?

MME. DUBONNET

But of course. You know, you were wise to come to the Ball. When one is feeling sad, the only thing to do is to try and forget.

POLLY

I shall never forget.

MME. DUBONNET

Courage, mon brave. In the meanwhile, why not enjoy yourself? Look, here are all your friends around you, so do not be
downcast.

The GIRLS *and* BOYS *surround her.*

OMNES

Hullo, Polly. [*Etc.*]

MAISIE

Hullo, Polly, I'm so glad you've come.

NANCY

We all missed you like mad, didn't we, chaps?

OMNES

Yes, we did, Polly. [*Etc.*]

POLLY

Thank you. It's so nice to know I've got some real friends.

ROLL OF DRUMS. *The* GARÇON APPEARS

GARÇON

Attention! Attention! Mesdames et Messieurs, asseyez vous, s'il
vous plait! We now present the rage of the Continent, Pépé and
Lolita, who are going to dance the Carnival Tango.

LADY B.

Revolting!

The assembly settle down with excited murmurs of 'The Carnival Tango,' 'Pépé and Lolita' etc. BOYS *and* GIRLS *clap.*

ENTER *the Specialty Dancers. They dance a Tango to the delight and astonishment of everybody except* LADY B. *and* GO OFF *to tumultuous applause.*

There is a general dispersal. POLLY *remains with* PERCIVAL; HORTENSE *draws* MADAME DUBONNET *aside.*

HORTENSE

Madame Dubonnet, I wish to have a little word with you about Mam'selle Browne.

MME. DUBONNET

Yes, Hortense? What is it?

HORTENSE

I fear she is wishing to leave the Ball already, but if you can persuade her to stay, I do not think she will regret it.

MME. DUBONNET

Very well, Hortense, I will do what I can.

HORTENSE

Merci, madame.

EXIT HORTENSE. MADAME DUBONNET *joins* POLLY *and* PERCIVAL.

MME. DUBONNET

You do not wish to dance, Polly?

PERCIVAL

I have already asked her myself, but she prefers not to.

MME. DUBONNET

Never mind. The night is still young. Let you and I have a little talk together.

POLLY

Very well, madame.

PERCIVAL *goes upstage.*

MME. DUBONNET

You know, Polly, when I look at you in that sweet costume, you remind me of a song I knew when I was a child.

POLLY

Do I? Can you sing it?

MME. DUBONNET

Yes, I think so.

> There is an old French legend
> That's set to an old French tune.
> It tells how Pierrot loves Pierrette
> Under a summer moon.
> Every night the lovers meet
> Just as the clock strikes nine.
> Then he gives her kisses sweet
> As vintage wine.
> But, alas, one fateful night
> Pierrette is forsworn,
> There she stands forlorn
> Till the cold grey dawn.
>
> Poor little Pierrette,
> Where's your Pierrot?
> Why are you all alone?
> You should be
> So fancy-free.
> Your heart should be high.

But instead
You hang your head
And try not to cry.

Poor little Pierrette,
You mustn't show
Your dream of love has flown.
Just keep on dancing
Till the dawn, and then
He may come back again.

At the end of the number, the others RE-ENTER. TONY
APPEARS *dressed as Pierrot and masked.* HORTENSE *runs to*
MADAME DUBONNET *and points him out excitedly. Every-
one is riveted.*

HORTENSE

Regardez, Madame Dubonnet. C'est Pierrot. Il est arrivé!

MME. DUBONNET

Look, Polly! Pierrot has not forgotten after all!

POLLY

Oh! [*putting on her mask*]
  TONY *comes down looking at all the ladies. He finds* POLLY.

TONY

May I have this dance, Pierrette?

POLLY

I'm afraid I can't dance with a stranger.

TONY

But I am Pierrot. You are Pierrette. Surely we are not strangers?

POLLY

But I don't know who you are.

TONY

Perhaps this will remind you. [*He kisses her*]

POLLY

It isn't—it isn't——

TONY

[*Removing his mask*] Yes, Polly, it's me.

POLLY

[*Removing hers*] Tony!

TONY

Polly!

LADY B.

Hubert! It's Tony! We've found him at last!

LORD B.

[*Going to him*] Tony! My boy! [*They embrace him*]

PERCIVAL

And who, may I ask, is this young man?

LORD B.

This, sir, is my son, the Honourable Tony Brockhurst.

POLLY

The Honourable Tony Brockhurst! Oh!

TONY

Yes, Polly, I'm afraid I am not a messenger boy after all. Can you forgive me?

POLLY

Oh, yes!

LADY B.

And who, may I ask, is this young woman?

PERCIVAL

This, madam, is my daughter. And I am Percival Browne.

TONY

Percival Browne, the millionaire?

POLLY

Yes, Tony. I'm afraid I've deceived you too. I'm not a secretary after all. Can you forgive me?

TONY

Of course, my darling! [*They embrace*]

MME. DUBONNET

La la, it seems that love is in the air tonight.

PERCIVAL

It is indeed. Polly, I too have some news.

POLLY

Have you, Daddy? How thrilling!

PERCIVAL

May I tell her, Kiki?

MME. DUBONNET

But of course. She should be the first to know.

PERCIVAL

Very well, then. Polly, Madame Dubonnet has just consented to become my wife.

BOBBY

Maisie! It's midnight—have you thought it over?

MARCEL

Et toi?

PIERRE

Et toi?

ALPHONSE

Et toi?

GIRLS

After due consideration we have come to the conclusion that the answer is unanimously—yes!

BOBBY

Swell—now how about that Charleston?

Everybody Charlestons to THE BOY FRIEND.

GRAND FINALE *with Balloons and Streamers.*

C U R T A I N